Decluttering the Closet

Jennifer Brunick

BookLeaf Publishing

Presentation by *BookLeaf Publishing*

Web: www.bookleafpub.com

E-mail: info@bookleafpub.com

ISBN: 9789357440028

First edition 2023

DEDICATION

To Michael, Corey, Morgaine, and Connor. You four are my whole library.

To Sarah. You, sister, are the other half that makes me whole. We don't work unless we're together.

Guys Not Dolls

When I was a kid, my cousins and I played Star Wars,
All the time.
I had all the Star Wars guys.
Guys not dolls, guys not dolls, GUYS NOT DOLLS
until I got older.
When they became collectible action figurines.
But if you had enough cousins around,
It's better to become the characters yourself,
We called it The Game with the same practiced sedateness,
Even if it had been months since we'd seen each other last
Rule #1: Never talk about the game.
When the parents would ask what we were doing, we'd say playing
Because they wouldn't get it anyway.
After delicate negotiations we'd
Morph into Skywalker or Hans Solo
flow into Leia, until the day of the metal bikini, see
When all bets are off
We'd all just play like that scene never existed
Lean far away because when you are 10 there is nothing cool about metal bikinis
Lean far away because when you are 40 there is nothing cool about metal bikinis
In fact, we'd play like no scene existed,
gifted with the ability to make up stories. Big fucking whoppers.
We invented fan fiction, no dice, no restrictions!

Rule #2 Follow the basic rules of play--no exception, meaning
Han Solo cannot just magically "get" the force. BT Dubs. (Sarah.)
Also, no replays. If you died the story starts over, or you became someone else, just like that, see through another someone's eyes
Arrive at the story as a completely new person
No earthen burden of the finality of death,
Protect your character as long as you can though.
Yoda was the only character above death,
You can't kill off the genius of that muppet,
However, CGI Yoda is free game. New rule.
Of course, you didn't get a light saber, at least not back then,
Because you had the force, which is cooler.
The hot grass under our bare feet became the frozen system of Hoth,
Sweating under my dad's old army jackets or robes
We'd kill imperial probes from the backs of our Tauntauns,
So Vader wouldn't be alerted of our presence.
Sliding our seventies shades—goggles--to the top of our heads,
To look through our electro-binoculars—toilet paper rolls,
Surveying the Arctic blasted landscape grimly.
Rescue Luke from the wampa, stop for lunch in the now bloody cave (PB&J).
Suddenly we could be in the Degobah system, decided on by the creator,
who was either me or John, he was tougher,

but I could bend a story like no other and welcomed additional suggestions,
Unless they were stupid
whatever our methods, we stayed in character and played for keeps all day and into the night.
Later, when we were supposed to be asleep,
we'd discuss high points and strategies
until one day we didn't have enough swagger
to keep fighting imaginary attackers without shame
and just like that we became grown up (sort of)
and The Game was over.
Life became all about gravity, keeping us grounded in reality
We lost the capacity to lie with such commitment.
But in the back of my head somewhere,
back there where bushes become bears
I think about who I'm coming back as.
And it will be night,
And there will be a lightsaber involved.
Because I'm still the creator.

Distraction

My library is (mostly) in the center of my house, like a heartbeat,
But the books slip out of the library like veins,
Coagulating into piles and pools of words
and everytime I stop working, when everything pulls me away I have to walk through
and see the picture of my Grammy on the bottom shelf,
staring at me from when she was only twenty
Black hair, blue eyes, red lips
Reminding me to get my shit done before I peek into the shelves
But there are days, I tell her, days like today when there are sights to seek out; thinks to think about
Not large ones, I assure her,
but a plethora of small loud ones
Black hair, blue eyes, red lips
like the bright yellow leaves outside the window
and the bright colored spines on the shelves
and the poem that is just right out of my reach
and there is no coffee in the house
And the cats are dancing on my papers
And there are ladybugs crawling across my ceiling
And tomorrow I have decreed it to be Buy -a - book day
She tells me, not for the first time, to ignore the distractions
She tells me, not for the first time, that I need to pay attention
ignore the interruptions within my interactions with the world

but the world is so big today, I say,
Black hair, blue eyes, red lips
The world is so big today
And sometimes that feels so loud and mean
Sometimes I feel like a faulty cog in a overly complicated machine
pushed into aggravated absolutes of thoughts I had ten minutes before they came to your mind--
--you, you root into me like I'm someone who can be fixed
Black hair, blue eyes, red lips
Like I'm a horrible mess.....Which is true
Like I lose everything.......Which I do
look, there is just--never--enough--time,
Its delicate strands too intangible to band together
Moments inflexible in their incurable need to march forward
The tighter I hold, the faster they slip away and fold into the cracks
Black hair, blue eyes, red lips
Which track through the lines on my fingertips
time does not linger; time does not grip desperately as it slips away from me,
biting playfully at my lower lip on its way away from me
You gave me time wrapped in brown paper packages tied up with string
Like Atropos of the Fates I cut it open to
create and pace concentric circles from the authentic center of my home
in order to retreat...
into my heartbeat

Facebook Friends With God

I'm Facebook friends with God now.
What the hell, I shrugged, already friended half my junior high,
most of which I didn't like in junior high . . .
And God is everything Hollywood has told us he is
An old white guy with a beard
And God is everything every religion has said he's not.
God is a liberal.
Factually speaking, that one part is a lie
—not the junior high part or the God as a liberal part,
But that I shrugged, see, that
I shrugged like I didn't stop for just a moment
and think about all the ramifications of friending God.
Question, is he a vengeful God?
Do I unfriend his holiness the Dali Lama to make her happy?
"Ye shall have no other Gods!"
It occurred to me that Grandma
might knock me upside the head for such blasphemy;
It occurred to me that it's about time God joined us in the 21st century.
Though mostly I thought about the ramification of the instant gratification of answers.
"Like" and I can run to Facebook and ask him where my keys are

"Like" and I can run to Facebook and ask him where
my phone is
"Like" and I can ask for do-overs—be kind rewind
Like when my mind moves faster than my mouth.
God reminds us that oxygen is free, but we are bound
to be forgetful of its bounty until it's gone.
And sounds like--Morgan Freeman.
I assume. I mean, it's not like I can hear him on
Facebook.
And sometimes I look on his page just to see the
selfies
Hoping to see him, David Foster Wallace and Elvis
during a century long rager
I wager will still be going on long after I get there
Just to stare at Mary playing rummy with Mark
Twain and Lucy
For cuz everyone loves Lucy and I wouldn't be
surprised
to watch people rub thighs with Jesus and Socrates
Socrates who now sees the light on the education of
women,
sends me to the greatest library . . .
Suddenly I am the new age Dante, minus the Catholic
regulation,
who is also there—no more stewing with political
retaliation for that dude.
Lighter mood, great food, coffee once a week with
Virgil never gets dull.
Chaucer says, "moss has grown over her notebooks.
Look how sad,
see the pen attached with cobwebs."

He begs for a story and I don't want to tell THE
Chaucer I can't see into that side of my
brain lately, the part of me left behind in North
Dakota.
Which is as close to hell as anyone can be really.
And while I'm trying to figure out what and how to
tell him, I realize that while no one
really dies in the pages of my books, I'm not looking
to live in the middle of someone else's story.
And I don't even know if she/he/it is real, besides
that Facebook deal.
But I wonder if God has a place in every city,
where he nods along with Pandora while she stands
in the kitchen in her socks
drinking juice from a box while its cats roam free at
his feet.
Me, I can't ever see through the mess, but I'm always
gonna wonder
Whether God was one of us
Just a slob like one of us.
But unless it can tell me why I can't sleep
And who I meet in my dreams that I don't keep
I think I'm just going to stick with trying to find me
in the pile of jointless words,
hollow like the bones of a bird
Put them together like legos into a poem of me,
deconstructed and decomposed from my barest
elements, evidence of
conscientious Mortality and practical unreality
Once, when I was driving to school at 4:30 in the
morning,

to assist in a senior prank, which I had nothing to do with if anyone asks,
a chicken ran out in the road and in answer a deer followed after,
chasing it to the other side, one after another, identical in gait,
thus answering at least one of the ecumenical questions that occasionally plague me
I am a chronically cosmic agnostic, I observe the universe and it just gets bigger
Reinforces my trust that truth is infinite, revealing itself in miniscule increments,
if at all, and you gotta accept that,
Except that if someone asks why the chicken crossed the road,
Now you got that one.
You're welcome.

I Wish I Wrote That

I write notes to myself on my hands,
sometimes so many by the end of the day
that the words dig in their nails and crawl up my arms
and wrists
and with minds of their own they coexist with books
and meetings
to secret greetings from gods I knew intimately one
thousand lives ago
and your very flesh shall be a poem
Walt Whitman whispers to me while I wash them off
like I knew him
and every time I feel that spoken my body opens up
into a totem;
feeling both wicked and wholesome
addicted and unaffected
there is a restricted section in that library
where the ink runs deep and
contrary to what you see and think
I still forget to remember
that book, that meeting, that greeting
but the center of my intentions are true
and what you see pressed into my palms are traces of
my people, from my day
like a living journal of jubilant
And I can wash away the external but they're still
living internal
right under my thin skin, look closer and see them
imprinted

One of these days I'm gonna go all long winded on myself,
writing words and phrases all over myself
scribing chatty across my chin
and just so there's no point of confusion, print
never thinks before she speaks across my lips
wide-awake snakes across my eyelids like a shadow because
I'll never outgrow hating all the time I lose sleeping
keeping secrets and yummy scrawled across my tummy
and luck right over my heart.
I'll write highfalutin across my forehead
and uppity on the tip of my nose
Sassy on my left hand, kinda artsy on my right
Wistful, whimsical and versed calligraphied up my right arm while
egotistical, digital and unpredictable are haphazardly scribbled on my left
and blessed…..emblazoned right across my chest,
just so everyone reads it,
so they know they're part of it.
Eventually and hopefully I'm becoming, literally, poetry.
And because poetry is potent stuff, like being happy,
it's a virus that's gonna spread like kindness

Mothering

He tells me to leave the hall light on and I comply
Because while darkness has a weight and the ability to multiply anyway,
one little night light slows it way down, at least long enough to shut your eyes for a while
There are times when I am spending all of my whiles looking for a one little light
And I lose sight of me in a world looking at me like a problem to be solved
Like him, I don't want to be the problem
Like him, uncertainty occasionally envelopes me in a wave and
I become the enclave in the now foreign territory of me
And while holding my breath, while waiting impatiently for the tide to go out,
I miss me.
So I leave the light on and recite silently and sacredly to myself
"You are enough."
"You are more than enough"
And I search for one tiny light
One droplet of a moment just for me to restore a balance

So when I say, you are enough for me just the way you are,
I meant it with my entire being though I know you are seeing something else

though I know you are feeling something else and I can't fix that for you,
though I really wish I could.
So go and deal with your wave, I'll be here when the tide moves on.
Then we will unclench our teeth and breathe together
beneath the weight of our own personal expectations self evaluations and observations
No abbreviations in the course of our determinations
Sometimes, this is just how it is
There will be days like this
We know there are a superfluous amount of days like this
Numerous days like this.

But there are other days, friend
Days where we didn't lose one thing, not even a pen
Days when nothing bad happens
Days where everything gets done, the desk stay relatively clean,
and we can sleep without a light on
because the nothing is so far away today
For today the nothing is far, far away and breathing happens just like magic
Like we don't even have to think about it
And we sit tight into this day and know that we can fake our way through the others
And everything is going to be okay, friend.
Everything is going to be okay

Pay Attention

Pay Attention
I drive too slow down the highway, see,
but fast enough for me
My chin flows back and forth in reply to music turned
up way too high
and I fly with my
whole arm out the window, fingers wide apart
catching air
having a momentary affair with the wind sailing through
my orange tipped fingernails
that just can't quite sink in
but I can feel the skin of the atmosphere placing me here
in this second
which is the next best thing because at that moment
I am present
to the farthest extent anyone can actually be present
because at that moment I can see straight through to
infinity
and I become the prayer on your lips,
the music that grips, moving your hips
stripping, and sucking down life to the marrow--
screw yesterday and tomorrow, I remain completely
today
my hero, impressed against you deep deeper in my chest
I'm gonna curl up and rest in this moment
I don't want to miss this moment
who lent itself to me when I was too busy going to see
where I went.

Y'all, I spend most of my time heading somewhere
other than here
or thinking about where I have to head, or want to head,
which means I'm already not here.
As soon as I think about leaving, the most present part
of me is already gone
and It's taken me years to realize the second you step
out of a moment
the second you step out of a poem or a thought
it's gone and you can't get that back.
No time to unpack, too busy believin' constant
movement equals purpose,
so American of us to not solve for X
when it intersects with why?
Cuz it's good medicine to climb into your own head
again
and chill with your muses, choosing your music.
So pay attention.
Sloooow.....down.
Turn it up way too loud.
And stick your whole arm--out the window.

Pocketful of

He's got pockets full of pieces that were once parts of a
whole
a dried up dragonfly with one wing
some mangled metal thing
a little plastic head of an action figure
a twig with the bark half peeled off
disfigured chocolates mashed, squashed and melted
a chunk of someone's driveway embedded with pebbles
a small slice of yellow pottery and a
fairly large quantity of bent and broken paperclips
all tokens--deemed essential enough to shove in his
pockets in that moment
I shrug and shove his pants in the machine and
pile up his things between various cleaners above the cat
food bowl
knowing I am a proponent of my own pockets full of parts
recollecting on my own pockets full of parts.
(I've had more time to collect)
unfinished parts and broken parts and
parts of whole things that may be or could be or will
never be
The collector in me always makes room.
I've got partial degrees, mangled majors and minors
A charred piece of friendship I ended out of personal
necessity,
reminding me that I miss the idea of it more than anything
else.

I’ve got three unfinished novels, thousands of poems undone
a string of teaching moments I didn’t have the time to utilize
a string of teachable moments I didn’t take the time to utilize
unactualized talents and unrealized dreams
I’ve got some baby teeth from all three of my babies
though I couldn’t tell you which one belongs to who
as they were haphazardly accrued in that blue box on the yellow shelf
because I am well aware of how creepy it is to save teeth.
I’ve got size nine Levi’s who hide in the back of my closet,
deposited just in case I ever get back there.
I have a spot where I place cords for charging electronic technology
I may or may not even own anymore.
Childish and clunky pottery created by my kids,
Fortune cookie fortunes who rang true, and
fortune cookie fortunes who don’t, but I wish them to be so
A steady flow of papers stack up from meetings that occurred a long time ago
I have books to finish reading, and books to start reading.
The cremated remains of my dog Marley in a surprisingly small box,
considering how large he was back when he was all together and breathing.
A pocket full of keys who have no home and appear to be breeding,
I have a small pile of bad habits broken,

A larger pile of bad habits unbroken,
A pocketful of words misspoken
A pilates DVD--unopened
Somewhere in there lies an abandoned Master's degree
Somewhere in there lies artsy-looking rocks looking to
artsy to toss
Pockets full of unintentionally stolen pens and lighters
Pockets full of words like writer and warrior
which make me feel both euphoric and uneasy
stashed in the place I peek into when it's difficult to
please me or when
I have the time and/or inclination
Pockets are simply the centralization of the shit that
refuses devaluation,
an edification offering personal illumination if one
chooses to look inside.
All of these little parts and pieces
percolate through to create the chaos of us and me;
if one chooses to see, we could save the world by turning
out our pockets
because knowledge is the basis of peace, there inside little
dusty boxes
where we recognize pieces of ourselves concealed and
confined
inside someone we never guessed held intimate
resemblances to us.
Pockets full of declarations to the worlds outside of us,
every notation and frustration bared to the worlds outside
of us;
Changing the world by turning out our pockets,
putting it piles outside the machine
where just anyone can see it

Mr. Old School Poetry Man

Sir, you kept me up all night and no,
Not in the way you're thinkin';
This isn't one of those kinds of poems;
It's a song of people; democracy of poetry
And I could see that you hated it
And I'm okay with that because
You hated my shit
passionately;
Which is the point of poetry for me:
I want blood and flesh meshed with tears

We all should fear language that pushes us to the edge of a precipice
we're not able to jump off yet;
We all should feel outraged at the shove
between the shoulder blades to a place
we aren't able to go yet;
so I am okay with the fact that you hated it.
And the joy of that is what kept me up;
Because like you,
I cut my teeth on Dickinson,
Had deep discussions with John Donne
And sexual fantasies over Whitman,
(Even though he was probably gay—its always the hot ones you know?)
so I see where you were coming from, son.

If I believed in a Christian God,
in my mind, he looks just like you,
Just like my Grandpa.
First thing--twinkly eyes
and definitely an accent…
Because God would never speak American.
And somewhere in there,
judgment.
Because he who sent his only son
and all that
Obviously God has seen some shit;
Rough bloody actions; warring factions;
Kissed girls, I imagine,
and as he pulled away
Probably uncomfortably missed society
And even as I disagree with you; I feel you;
And even as I bleed on the page
or tell a story
I see poetry in the air around me;
Sometimes--it just stops me;
White apple blossoms
and waxy green leaves
Leaning against a purple night sky
Like lovers wrapped up into each other;
Brother, believe me when I say
I feel that with you;
Sometimes images are so true
my chest constricts
Because what I see is
almost too honest
If I believed in a Christian God
I would say that image is her slam poetry

Cuz I envision that
she could throw some shit down
in this word scrimmage.

I have met others like you and found
There is no such thing as
Old world and New World…
It's the same old world
with different accessories;
Same stories different cast
Same clothes different cut
Same substance different shape
And we all slip together into last judgment.

So even if you never relent on your stance
Even if you never repent your sins,
Like God, I still hold poetry at where
it begins and ends

The Universe

A cavernous universe smells like old books and
tastes of dark coffee with
three shots of espresso,
perhaps even more-so within the mysterious nothing
between the letters.
It sounds like the buzzing of constant and serious
thoughts as the words,
like stars, clot together and weave a constellation,
a convocation of tales.
Stories compose the universe, not atoms,
like superimposed Legos of reactions and
find-out-what-happens leaves
fairy dust on your philosophies,
sometimes, having grown weary of theory,
I put my hand right up to the night sky and
imprint my own stories into the stars.
Centuries . . . or years . . . or three days from now
people will read my destiny across the rooftops of the
universe
singing in unison, a fusion of opportunity and
evolution.
I believe the universe will deliver everything you put
out there
So be-wareful of the gravitational pull as you write
your story out of thin air,
know you are capable of repair,

almost nothing is permanent though everyone is
essentially terminal;
strange particles who float
until they find that thing they never realized they
were looking for
until that very moment they see it
until that very moment they say it
and the word tastes distant and infinite as it rolls off
your tongue because you are an instrument
within the endlessness of the universe and reverse
does not exist here
There is frozen or forward in an ocean of moments
and ferocious commotion.
--You have to learn to listen--
to the deep, dark quiet between the letters where the
climate offers seconds of silence
and the droplets of the atmosphere tastes like dark
coffee and chocolates.

Vampires Don't Suck OR That Time I Read Twilight

Vampires Don't Suck
I've got a dirty secret.
After many years of strictly literature,
I've met a vampire
and acquired a little crush.
Don't try to rush away.
You say you can do better
and you most certainly can.
The writing lacks…everything,
The editing…nonexistent.
The vocabulary tried to be an accomplishment
…and missed.
Question: If a thesaurus falls in a forest would
Stephenie Meyer misuse all of those words too?
You assume that you can just choose to not pursue
this novel, but it accepts no refusal.
Kisses you softly on the collarbone, phones you
every night like a lover, cradles you like no other.
THEN GOES IN THE FOR THE KILL!!
But he can't cuz he loves you still,
But the Twilight bite now exists, time mists into
nothingness . . .
Screw the lesson plans, I've gotta get through book two!
Who's kids are you?? Me, I'm single through book
three.

I can't afford book four…Lord damn thy shitty job
market.
Fuck it. I'll get the movie . . .from somebody, anybody!
Look at me, I'm falling!
Edward save me.
Let me ride on your back like a spider monkey!
Let me watch when you light yourself up like a
Christmas tree!
See, you touched my inner apple, forced it to touch me.
And Damn it! I believe! Virginia, vampires do exist!
But wait. I feel I missed….something.
Why do these books make me sing?
Dost thou this ring perchance of something evil this way
comes??
I say she fell, descended into hell! Had a conversation
with Dante and Faust,
a conglomeration doused with….Satan!!
So it's not me who's lost all literary credibility;
see, the devil made me read it.
I mean it. It's like crack!
Read the first three chapters and then just try and stop!
I lack the will power because Stephenie Meyer
snatched it away from me.
It's so scary; I haven't felt this alive since Harry.
And the witch says she's not going to write book five!
And I sayeth Bitch! You owe me!

The Alphabet

A Poem to those I recently unfriended and/or blocked:
Adulation of able bodied Americans acting
badass bitter by backing boys in blue-black suits
bitching about brown people
BLOCKED
who are
caterwauling christian cacklers only capable of captions
against crying children
who are
dangerously damning and dancing on those who
survived death to
eat economics and edicts
from fucking fearmongering faux news famous for
galvanizing gangrenous ghastly gabble
who are
handing her hell in a handbasket with heartless hands
and not even a hovel to home
images in instant-time that isolate and identify our
inability to act and icy indifference
--just in case they might be Isis--
--and willing to struggle for at least three years through
paperwork and background checks
as a refugee before being allowed on American soil--
but I digress.
who are
jeering, judging, jealously guarding and jawing about
Jesus while
keen on the Ku-bbal-uh, but scared shitless of the Koran

love loading lubricated lies and living large, lynching
behind a computer screen
mewing malignantly macho modified manifestos
manifesting manipulations and misrepresentations of
Muslim men, women and children
who move because their manger was blown up and we
won't open the inn.
Offensive openers objurgate old phrases,
"I'm not trying to be racist, but…"
Participating in pandemic paranoid paramilitary-thrown
pitchforks into a
quagmire quoting quarrels that quell any questions that
might lead to quintessential kindness.
Rapacious rabid relicts resurface like reconverted and
reused yellow
stars. Scowling saints sing in the sanitized safety of the
states and stand in scarecrowish and
tasteless tailpipes of terror as time watches them sleep
on streets and trains to nowhere.
Unfriend the ubiquitous and ugly umbrellas uniting
them against
victims whose lives vaporized before their eyes
while we the people wax on about freedom, wading
through once Native lands
Xeroxed Xanadu yearning for zealous zones
where everyone is the same.

Story Maker

When I worked at a nursing home I used to give stories away to dementia patients
like my kid gives me dandelions, with both carelessness and my whole heart.
Stories dipped in milk chocolate lies and wrapped in truth, set gently on cracked palms.
I washed their faces while their words fell like drizzle and they searched
the darkened corners of their minds for bits of anything
Crumbs of moments
Flashes of faces
First fear then fury, normally directed at me
Hey, I said. Hey. Do you remember that time?
When you were far away in Philadelphia and you got drunk with Walter Cronkite?
Right, you nodded. On business. I hated that guy.
I know; I nodded back. That's why you hit him.
Kronkite was an ass, you growled and waited with palms wide open.
I went on, describing a little corner bar with very little light and peanut shells carpeting the floor,
just a block from your hotel. You were there, missing your wife, wishing you didn't work so much
Marie, you added, reminiscing with me.
She bought new curtains while I was gone. Expensive curtains.
Yeah! And in walks Walter Cronkite, hanging his hat, crunching on the peanut shells.

And he was loud.
Yeah! Because you hate that and because it was just you, the bartender and the quiet,
but then he was suddenly there, laughing and likeable and horrible and all at once too much
He bought me a drink like he was so important.
Yeah! But you were both there, talking at each other through the mirror behind the bar,
getting drunker; he called you a free thinker
Why? You interrupted. I cupped your chin to wash your neck. I don't know, I said.
And that part is true, I really didn't know yet.
I don't know, I said again, but he was going on about FDR's foreign policy while you and Marie were having a preemptive argument in your mind over the new curtains for the window above the sink.
I showed him a picture of Marie--
And then there was a pause and he looked at me for the end, leaning forward in his chair,
waiting for the rest of his story
And he said she wasn't so much, touching your back while he laughed and you got mad--
Damn right, he said, leaning forward, completely present in the trajectory of this memory.
You knocked him on his ass, I finished. Laid him right out, I said, and the thread of that moment
became a component of an image,
the vision of a drunken, flushed Cronkite face floated between us
smelling of cigarettes, cheap scotch and peanuts.
I liked the blue curtains better, you admitted after a few minutes

I'm gonna tell her when she comes today.
I didn't want my answer to be that she died four years ago of breast cancer because I could see only that the Cronkite memory was better
and as I dried your face, I lied. Again.
I said a little carelessly and with my whole heart,
Marie's buying you shirts today, remember?
And you could see that too because Marie sure likes to spend money.

Infinity

So she points to the entwined infinity symbol
necklace through the glass window
It's on sale for $2.99
And she says whimsically,
but unaware that she is so
"Infinity is trending now."
And depending on whom you are,
spending $2.99 on infinity…
Well, that's a good deal, so I don't laugh
though it tickles the corners of my lips
Which curve up to
catch all of her best intentions
Listen, I see infinity everywhere I look here
Rooms filled with rugs and books and cats
and poetry assure me
But my proclivity for aesthetics forced to coexist with
the messiness of all of our love
—look closer
Little stories jumbled into precarious piles
within the rooms about our house
Pink headphones slide swiftly to the floor when
He drops his shiny plastic snakes
haphazardly on my desk
It's anarchy when earrings and bangle bracelets
Find their way next to homeless fishing lures and
nuts and bolts (naturally) residing
In that drawer where nothing specific goes,
so everything does,

Deciding that Mortal Kombat, Gods of war
and Twilight can lie together on the floor
At least while we eat. Or longer.
I see my cup half full--of cold coffee--
kissed with the stain of my lipstick
Sitting peacefully with an empty
bottle of nail polish remover
And cotton dried into a burr smeared
with orange lacquer which
Serves as a reminder to stop at the store
Your dirty socks on the floor
with one Ninja turtle shoe,
So small in comparison
Perfection in imperfections
A tiny mili-section in the ludicrous
vastness of the universe
We are particles belonging to the miracle
of this precarious atom
These tiny plastic guns, butterfly scarf and fingernail
clipper all part of some precious,
brief experience we forget to think about again
A variance to the norm formed firmly into a new
norm for just that moment—look closer
At the rhythm of cat toys sprinkled liberally over the
carpet, let the pile of unshelved books
Look askance toward the PlayStation 3,
--Books can be so judgy--but even they see we all
weirdly belong
We are the composers and love—love is supposed to
be messy y'all,
Fleshy and crazy
Here, in the middle of infinity.

There For You

There are things I need to tell you before you leave, things
you need to know.
So stop.
Just stop for a minute.
Stop making plans and stop packing.
Stop boxing up your comics and hero clicks
and Pokemon cards.

Stop getting taller than me.

I just need a minute to think. I just need a minute.
There are things I need to tell you before you leave.
You have been counting the days,
but I don't think I ever saw 18 coming.
Eighteen years hit me like a brick wall knocking the air from
my lungs. It's pulling you away from me and
my life is so entwined with yours the pull of it pulls
the thin skin of my heart away until I am raw inside.
So just stop.
Stop for a minute and let me catch my breath and
stop the bleeding.
I need to tell you that even when you weren't,
you were the perfect boy.
I need to tell you that I loved your punk music and passion
and protests.
But I hated your Mohawk and am relieved we've moved past
this hair decision.

I need to tell you that even though I was 10 days away from
my seventeenth birthday when you were born,
even though I was just a girl,
even though all of that,
I loved you like a real live
grown up person.
I need to tell you to stay away from credit cards.

I need to tell you to call me every other day or at least
answer the cell phone I am paying for or I will start
calling your friends to make sure you are not dead in a ditch.

I need to tell you that I believe in the amazing person you
have become.
I need to tell you that I want you to experience
love and
college and
freedom and
your very own mistakes and
your very own successes.
And college.
Did I mention college?

I need to tell you that you were my
Very First Perfect Poem.
I need to tell you it's okay to leave and embrace your life and
never look back.

Except for my phone call every other day.

I need to tell you to ask if you need anything

because it has always been a privilege to be
there for you.
I need to tell you all this and more and I will.

I just need a minute.

Little Goddess

You are the fruit of my feminine ideology.
My Little Goddess breaths in Juliet and Beatrice from the womb,
dallies with Diana and Nancy Drew,
runs with the Garcia Girls and Ramona Q.

My Little Goddess rubs shoulders with the March girls,
singing with Alice, Sidda and Anne of the Gables Green,
my Little Goddess your
grace is felt and seen.

Little Goddess, you were conceived within the pages of
my favorite books.

You were the end result of my secret fairy dreams,
I kept your baby spirit safe inside a walnut shell, covering
you with a single, soft petal from a perfect pink rose.

I saved my favorite looking glass just for you,
I sought the most secretest of secret gardens,
the most Mad Hatter-est and Cheshire Cattiest tea,
for you are the fruit of my feminine ideology.

Little Goddess, here's a little Pandora's box with
a shiny red apple to take on a ship,
a Trojan ship,
free Helen
and Penelope

For you are the fruit of my feminine ideology.

Little Goddess, here is the fullest pale moon, your own
noble steed,
dolls draped in pink, and a
soft quiet corner in which to read.

My whole life has had me
trying to unlock the
key of my female-ness,
what it means to be a woman.
I studied at the feet of
Walker and Alcott.
I picked the brain of
Angelou and Byatt.

I knew their was a power,
a heart beat of half the world,
enflaming the other
if it gets too loud.
I can hear it on the street,
hear it in the pages of my
books on the shelves,
whispering me forward.

And then.

And then they put you in my arms all pink and perfect and
I knew then I would push you forward as my mother
pushed me and her mother push her.

Because that is what we do and

I never really knew that until you.
Which is to say, Little Goddess, that I never knew me.

You are the fruit of my feminine ideology.

For Cuz

Baby, your poetry makes me smile and I want to be
five right along with you;
your raw spirit never touched as such by the
civilization of the corporation of kindergarten and
while I gotta let it happen,
six is tappin' at my door,
I gotta tell you, I adore the before.
Even though I look forward to the silence cuz you
can run for days and need bigger things to explore.
You're an atomic pile of energy and though you make
me tired,
Your poetry makes me smile.

With six in sight you wear a batman cape everywhere
you go
Saving the day, not misbehaving but performing
dramatic rescues,
a climatic point of your very own; now that I am
grown,
I am content to just be
present for your turn.
This is your point of no return,
In these few days without homework and back packs
and
lunch out of paper sacks and talk of other things. Of
shoes and ships and sealing wax
And cabbages and kings

You move so fast I swear you have wings and your
poetry sings, your poetry sings,
I see love in your grimy face,
Ache when you race to kiss me first; my heart bursts,
miss you already, there's just enough to steady you as
your
world spins by me,
you feel flatulence is funny
flying laughing spinning crazy
"for cuz it smells how butt looks!"
And your poetry makes me smile.

You find fantastic stories in all the corners of your
world,
Told your daycare friends the mound of dirt outside
the fence
Has long since been a sacred burial place for an owl
"And then the wolf killed it and ate it and buried da
bones and da blood."
Your friends stopped hanging out by that part of the
fence
since the incident. And even as I fielded questions
from concerned teachers and mad moms,
I was glad your brain
maintains such an imagination,
a fantastical inclination towards
six impossible things
before breakfast.

Soon you're gonna have to do something;
there will be no more nothing,
They don't let you.

So do nothing while you still can,
Superman, believe in everything until you can't;
And know your poetry makes me smile, kid.
Before you rid yourself of childish things,
I will cling to this time for cuz your poetry sings
and when the Wild Things
Are squatting under your bed you said "but dey will
kill me with der bones and blood
And we gotta tell someone!"
And even as I solemnly swear to never let the
monsters eat you,
Invoking the power of Batman, Spiderman and
Grayskull
Your poetry makes me smile.

Neurodivergent

Attention Deficit Disorder means my mind follows a different order ADD to more than an adequate degree that's me a cassette recorder on fast forward it's turning right when you mean to go…that other way. I mean to say my mind's light is on there's just so much of it I'm on lickety split when everyone else is moving
Too Slow
I need to flow. Though I empathize with your inability to follow me I lack predictability I'm nothing but mobility--Have you seen that new book I got…by that guy, I can't find that anywhere….I swear--I know you just care when you tell me to be mellow but you're a nice calm blue to my canary yellow. I read Dickens watch Tom and Jerry and fold laundry while the plot the plot thickens jot down lines of my poetry I could have otherwise forgot, my mind's got its own symmetry beauty in disorder no assumed border on what is a possibility constant apostasy part of my idiosyncrasy, I don't need you to get it, that bit of me, see I own it, can live with it thrive in it my mind is no aberration I choose no medication, caffeine takes the edge off because my day can get mean without it, but I got it, baby, I got it. And I know I don't sleep but four or five hours a night, right, I get that, but I can't let your worries eat at me, see, there is so much to get done before I sleep and if I work with only the sun I'll fall behind in the

long run. Look, I don't just read one book at a time; I read 12 at light speed and you disagreed with my methods but as my thoughts drop like weeds on overdrive I need to revive and revitalize by hopping to the next, mad respect to those who can do only one at a time but that is not the way roll---
You know what sounds really good? Fruit Roll up's. I haven't had one of those in forever--I never sit still for long; I'll try to belong and get along, but make me sit for more than an hour things go real sour for me, see I need to be moving, improving what I think so I can say—Hey—do you know how many ADD kids it takes to change a light bulb? You wanna ride bikes? I like. Sometimes I find myself seeking syllables so speaking doesn't get wrapped around my teeth untapped words become absurd underneath my tongue ADD one, me none. But son, that's okay. My mind will fly astray because it's unlined but inclined to try anything new, look at a different point of view, ideas long overdue--shit I need to get my licensed renewed--I'm always 5 to 10 minutes late on the dot, cognitive state…never mind lost my train of thought….You wanna figure me out and I don't doubt you come from a good place but baby brace yourself—I don't get me all the time either so it's fine that neither can you, just know my life is better with you there, and living with me can be unfair, as I fly around your feet are firmly on the ground. When life goes askew I picture a plethora of fairies speaking poetry swooping in to the rescue attracted to my positive aura. If you ask them, they will come, and you like, um, why don't we just use part of savings

account, not to interfere with the fairy story, but I don't think Richard Cory or Shakespeare are gonna help with this gas bill…still you-

Wait. When did we get a savings account?

Plant Assassination or Perennial Manslaughter

Rest in peace little viney plant thing,
rest in peace.
Death by dehydration
A Goddess creation
Death through lack of communication;
see I've had poetry on my mind, I've had poetry on my mind,
Didn't mean to be unkind, I've had poetry on my mind.
There are times when the verbs possess me, when the nouns bless me, the words coalesce and caress and there is a creative excess and
I must profess that I like it. and it must be said that I don't care, you there. Little viney plant thing all withered away beyond resuscitation,
Martyred salvation, I don't care.
How, you gasp, do my offspring survive, my cats stay alive?
They tell me it's time to eat.
How simple is that?
It's a possessive passive aggression,
A clinical depression without question. The path towards true hydration and fluid sensation,
protect your population.
Open up your whiny little plant mouth and remind me to water you.

Who do you think you are?
Looking at me all sad, and dead---but
still there. Still there, dangling your little death carrot
an argument not without merit.
I don't care.
All around me there is a triage of destinations not yet
taken
Goals not yet gained, projects abstained, papers
maintained
And I can't care little plant thing.
I can't care.
My masters is stowed under the bed,
due to financial constraints.
A blank canvass lies in the corner waiting for my
paints, hair to be braided, papers to be graded.
There are books unread and poems unwritten. There
is a young man struggling be a grown up, a young
girl pretending to be a woman and a little boy
climbing up the walls.
And I can't care little plant thing, I can't care. But I
do wish you this.
May your next life grant you bliss.
May you find a woman who loves dirt. A man who
sees poetry in you
A human you'll warm to as she pulls you through.
But I can't care.
I can't.

Reverend Chuck

Speak the Bugs Bunny.
Speak the Road Runner.
Speak the Taz, man, speak the Taz.
Cuz sometimes I am Junior,
The little geek chicken
with the mother who never
knows what's going on.
With the glasses and inability and/or refusal
to
be who this world wants me to
be. And where everything is and can be
found in a book on the shelf and this
comforts
me in my self created bubble.

Cuz sometimes my ADD rears its ugly head and I am
Porky. And I have so many words I can't
hold them in
my mouth in such a way to spit them out in
the right order
and they fall to the ground in jagged broken
shards and I scramble
to collect them, glue the fragile letters
together and find my
thoughts. I am reduced to only a few
bloodied words in front of people
who need no caffeine or doctor prescribed
narcotics to carry

a thought from their brain to their mouth.

Cuz sometimes I am the coyote. I am the coyote with my dream just
out of my reach, just at my fingertips but not quite there, not
quite there, just one more thing and one more thing. And in spite of
my effort and all those Acme products I keep falling short
and I hold my sign high "Crap!" it says, as I fall from that cliff again
and again and I get up again and again waiting for that anvil
to drop on my head and I hardly care at all.

Cuz sometimes I am the Roadrunner. And I am cruising so well and
so fast that nothing can catch me. There is no anvil for the
Roadrunner. No faux painted wall of scenery he can't run
through. Because he is moving way to fast to stop and look
at the scenery. Just move, move, move onto that next big
bowl of birdseed baby.

Cuz sometimes I am Bugs Bunny saying hey what's up doc in that cool ass way
with that cool ass carrot and that calm, cool ass way of

getting lost, taking that wrong turn at
Albuquerque and just going
with that flow, moving with that flow,
fighting that bull and just
shaking himself off after getting knocked on
his butt. "I hope you
know this means war" he says and get right
into that game, dressing
in drag and singing that opera until any
opposition at all just lies down
and gives in.

So speak the Bugs Bunny, speak the Road Runner,
speak the little geek chicken, speak something other
than Sponge Bob.   Please.

And I am not going to say "that's all folks."

The penis doesn't age like the vagina.

In the nursing home I washed old flesh
carefully--so it wouldn't tear.
"Don't worry." Don would
sigh. I could hear the whistling whine in his lungs. "It
doesn't work anymore." He assured me as though he used
to be Dangerous--thousands of women scarred--running,
screaming in terror at the sheer size of
his cock. It used to be a cock. Now it is just a penis. For
lack of a smaller word.
It has shrunk
down to a
nub, a
pencil
sharpened
too many
times
and when he stands to
piss his scrotum hangs down to his knees. His wrinkles
distinguished, his body
portly, he has matured--But his penis is old. Wrinkled.
Unattractive. He gazes at it, laugh lines dimming and
I watch him mourn for it.

Irene weighs 72

pounds. Her one breast hangs down to her soft belly. "I have a 38 long." She laughs. Sometimes when she is on the toilet her
bladder falls half out of her. It is smooth and pinkish purple like a plum and I cup it with a gloved
hand, waiting for the nurse to come put it back. "It's all those babies." We chat as I support her insides on the outside. "We used to have so many." She has ten children who
never visit. Her bones are transparent because of menopause. She has had varicose veins since
her 30's. Her skin is wrinkled. The lack of estrogen
has given her a prominent moustache. However.
Her Vagina--ageless.
Masterpiece Pussy. A Georgia O' Keefe in repose. Their organs are dying and systems are shutting down. But there is a
piece of Irene who still
looks like Irene.

And when my flesh is old and begins to tear and
my organs begin to die and my systems are shutting down and I
am growing my moustache and my insides began
to fall to the outside and my breasts slip down to my
belly. When I am old. Wrinkled. Unattractive.

There will be that piece of me.
A piece of me who still
looks like me.
And I am wildly grateful to be a woman.

why Homer smells like fall

I am trying to read on the warm front steps
& the Manchild on his skateboard
calls "Mom watch!" & I slip my finger between the pages
& he flips his back wheels to the front & does it again &
again & going faster spinning crazy down the road & I hope
a car doesn't fly over the hill--"it's a oneeighty
endover!"--& make him no more & while I watch for
looming death Boo gives me a perfect blood red leaf with
his chubby sticky fingers & I say "thank you" & slide it
between the pages & he says "thank you" & smiling with
his entire body he picks his nose & places it on my palm
like a semiprecious stone & I wait until he isn't looking
before I wipe it off & the FaireeQueen wearing Wal-Mart
wings wants me to spin her crazy & I do & Boo
wants a turn & we are all spinning crazy at the same time &
later that night I
have to step outside into air that has begun to chill & my
breath is suspended in space as I exhume my book from the
pile of dead leaves and that is why Homer smells like fall.

www.ingramcontent.com/pod-product-compliance
Lightning Source LLC
Chambersburg PA
CBHW051737130826
49812CB00033B/898
* 9 7 8 9 3 5 7 4 4 0 0 2 8 *